Electricity Storage

Look at the battery.

We can keep electricity

in the battery.

3

Look at the little battery.
We can keep electricity
in the little battery.

5

Look at the big battery.
We can keep electricity
in the big battery.

7

Look at the flat battery.

We can keep electricity in the flat battery.

9

Look at the round battery.

We can keep electricity

in the round battery.

11

Look at the tall battery. We can keep electricity in the tall battery.

Look at the tiny battery.

We can keep electricity

in the tiny battery.

15

Look at these batteries.

We can keep electricity

in these batteries too.